MINDFULLY ME

MINDFULLY ME:

*30 Days to a Life of Peace
and Tranquility*

MARICHAL MONTS

XULON ELITE

Xulon Press Elite
2301 Lucien Way #415
Maitland, FL 32751
407.339.4217
www.xulonpress.com

Exulon ELITE

© 2020 by MARICHAL MONTS

All rights reserved solely by the author. The author guarantees all contents are original and do not infringe upon the legal rights of any other person or work. No part of this book may be reproduced in any form without the permission of the author. The views expressed in this book are not necessarily those of the publisher.

Unless otherwise indicated, Scripture quotations taken from the Holy Bible, New Living Translation (NLT). Copyright ©1996, 2004, 2007 by Tyndale House Foundation. Used by permission of Tyndale House Publishers, Inc.

Scripture quotations taken from The Message (MSG). Copyright © 1993, 1994, 1995, 1996, 2000, 2001, 2002. Used by permission of NavPress Publishing Group. Used by permission. All rights reserved.

Scripture quotations taken from The Living Bible (TLB). Copyright © 1971 by Tyndale House Foundation. Used by permission of Tyndale House Publishers Inc., Carol Stream, Illinois 60188. All rights reserved.

Scripture quotations taken from the English Standard Version (ESV). Copyright © 2001 by Crossway, a publishing ministry of Good News Publishers. Used by permission. All rights reserved.

Scripture quotations taken from the Contemporary English Version (CEV). Copyright © 1995 American Bible Society. Used by permission. All rights reserved.

Scripture quotations taken from The Holy Bible, Berean Study Bible (BSB). Copyright ©2016, 2018 by Bible Hub. Used by Permission. All Rights Reserved Worldwide.

Scripture quotations taken from the King James Version (KJV) – public domain.

Scripture quotations taken from the Holy Bible, New International Version (NIV). Copyright © 1973, 1978, 1984, 2011 by Biblica, Inc.™. Used by permission. All rights reserved.

Scripture quotations taken from the Christian Standard Bible. (CSB). Copyright © 2017 by Holman Bible Publishers. Used by permission. All rights reserved.

Printed in the United States of America.

Paperback ISBN-13: 978-1-66280-346-8
Hardcover ISBN-13: 978-1-6628-0347-5
eBook ISBN-13: 978-1-6628-0348-2

Dedication

I would like to dedicate this book to Auntie Nat. I am so grateful, privileged and honored to be your nephew. I will carry you in my heart until the day that I die. So much of who I am is because of you. Thank you for the years of laughter. I still believe God!

I'd also like to acknowledge the over 250,000 Americans (at the time of this writing) and over 1,250,000 members of the human race who were taken from us due to COVID-19 and the over 10,000,000 Americans and over 50,000,000 members of the human race who have been infected with this devastating illness. I pray that God gives you total healing and His precious peace.

I'd also like to thank every peaceful protester around the world who believes that our world can be better. Your combined voices are reaching Heaven and change is imminent. Let us keep praying and working for the peace that only He can give.

TABLE OF CONTENTS

Prologue ix

1: Persistence Connects You 1
2: Actions And Beliefs 5
3: Appreciate People 9
4: Timing Is Everything 13
5: Your Struggle Is Your Story 19
6: You Have Everything That You Need .. 23
7: Quiet Is Refreshing. Quiet Is Good ... 27
8: Learning Lifetime Lessons 31
9: Right Now Is Good 37
10: Peace…The Perfect Place 41
11: Exhale…Again! 45
12: Watch Words. Learn Words. 49

13: Shut Off Default Mode 55
14: Worry Is Sin 59
15: Perceive Temporary And Terminal 63
16. It's Only A Test 67
17. Tears Legitimize You 73
18. Prayer Really Works 77
19. Miracles Still Happen 81
20. Keep Feeling This Moment 85
21. Sitting With The Sovereign 91
22. That Is Their Choice 95
23. Destruction and Construction 99
24. Music Manifests Miracles 103
25. Sacrifice Superficial Subjects 109
26. It Took A Long Time 113
27. All Means All 117
28. Being Benevolent Blesses 121
29. Everything Wasn't A Lie 127
30. Go For Broke 131

Epilogue 135

Prologue

At the outset of COVID-19, the worst pandemic to hit the United States in 100 years, I immediately went into super pastor mode. I took to social media and told people that if they didn't come out of this season with some product indicating their creativity and uniqueness, they were wasting their life. I insisted that they didn't need more time, but more vision. And then what I thought would be 3 or 4 weeks of being quarantined, turned into over 4 months. I yelled at my television nightly at the ineptitude of the current Republican administration and remember getting increasingly numb and somber when the United States of America reached 100,000 deaths. Now, this was really unprecedented. All of this coupled with more and more Black people being murdered and the images of these tragedies constantly flooding social and traditional media caused me to emotionally shut down. I was grateful for Zoom when I needed to meet with people, but then I got Zoomed out. And I realized that the super pastor was exhausted, burned out, worn, and about to come out of COVID-19 empty handed. So I'm sharing with you some of the meditations of my heart. I share them because even though this pandemic has worn me thin, I still have peace, a peace that surpasses even my own understanding.

1.

Persistence Connects You

I would like to start with this simple, age old encouragement. Persistence is critical when trying to accomplish anything. I start here because so many people have asked me what is the most important lesson that I've learned after 25 years of pastoring The Citadel of Love.

J. Don Garner was an amazing friend and churchman who taught me a simple principle. If you want people to come to church, make sure that YOU show up. When they see that you are serious, then they will be serious. While he is at home with the Lord now, I never forgot those words.

Whatever it is that you desire to do, you must continue to work on it over and over. When it gets easy, that is the time reimagine your routines and go at it from another perspective. But your persistence is the chord that connects you to every winner in history. Every great human being has struggled with heartache, pain, disappointment and especially financial setbacks. Be that as it may, you must find joy in going back to your dream even when it is easier to walk away. A simple knowledge of history will show you how great people have experienced lows, depressions, divorces and have been cheated, abused and rejected. What made them great, more than their gift or talent, is the fact that they refused to quit.

What do you really desire to do? Where do you want to go with your life? What have you been dreaming about creating? Everything and everyone will not work with you to make it happen. But if you believe it in your soul, and you stay persistent, you will win. That is the kind of effort that God rewards. You were created by the Master Creator and when you refuse to quit, creativity must emanate from your being. Just don't stop. Your persistence is going to pay off.

> *With all this going for us, my dear, dear friends, stand your ground. And don't hold back. Throw yourselves into the work of the Master, confident that nothing you do for Him is a waste of time or effort*
> *—I Corinthians 15:58 (MSG)*

Mindfully Me

TODAY I WILL:

_____

_____

_____

_____

_____

_____

_____

_____

_____

_____

_____

_____

_____

_____

_____

_____

_____

_____

2.
Actions And Beliefs

In order to really know peace, it becomes imperative that one recognizes the absence thereof. That means we must be honest with ourselves. And while it may be difficult and often uncomfortable, telling yourself the truth about yourself and embracing it will only lead you to a deeper place of genuine spirit. Unfortunately, when we are consumed with the applause of the crowd, we will become performance driven. The satisfaction that comes from the noise of the crowd, however, is temporary or nominal at best. It is also addictive. Unfortunately, unhealthy addictions usually lead us to act incongruent with who we were intended to be. Our wonder is dimmed when under the influence of anything other than God's true Spirit.

There is a persistent war within us when the things that we are doing don't connect to what we really believe. So when we are acting for the crowd from a less than sterling place, there is a clear and present frustration that is debilitating. And you can do it for a long time and be considered a professional by those who don't know you. But when the lights are off and the crowd is gone, you know that you are miserable. You look around and see so many others who are walking in their personal peace while if feels as if a simple inner quietness eludes you.

Simply put, something has to change, or the misery will lead to a wasted life. The spiritual sparring that you are experiencing will only dissipate when your actions are tightly matched with your beliefs. When you are living and acting on what you really believe, the internal struggle will truly cease to exist, and the external noise of the crowd will no longer be necessary for satisfaction. You will sleep differently when you make sense of this concept. So do the hard work to make what you really believe connect with your actions. The hard work…

> *Don't copy the behavior and customs of this world, but let God transform you into a new person by changing the way you think. Then you will learn to know God's will for you, which is good and pleasing and perfect."—Romans 12:2 (NLT)*

Mindfully Me

TODAY I WILL:

_____

_____

_____

_____

_____

_____

_____

_____

_____

_____

_____

_____

_____

_____

_____

_____

_____

_____

3.
Appreciate People

Let's face it. People are a trip. They will love you one day and hate you the next (or in some cases just a few hours later). I am always baffled how people can be married for countless years, give the world beautiful children, build wealth and business together and then try to destroy each other in divorce court. Or how about the new person on the job who you took under your wing and showed them all that they needed to know in order to succeed, and then you find out that all along they were secretly undermining you to anyone in authority who would listen. There was a song when I was growing up about telling a friend a secret and then they told their friend and they told their friend, until everyone knew what you thought was a secret. Yes, people are something else.

However, instead of going into a shell like a turtle and never speaking to anyone ever again or hating everyone who ever hurt you, appreciate every person who has ever crossed your path. The same God who rains on the just and the unjust created them too. Appreciate them for the time that they were in your life. Appreciate the lessons that they taught, the ones that made you cry as well as the ones that made you grow. You see tears are critical for growth. Tears only mean that you are alive. The first thing that the doctor does when you arrive on the scene is cause you a little pain with a little spanking to make you cry. And then the journey of learning begins.

We do not have the luxury of taking anyone or anything for granted. Doing so could very easily lead to one's expiry. Just as you have a purpose for being on this earth right now, every person who you experience is important to the

Appreciate People

fullness of your journey on earth. How you handle them will determine how quickly your life is filled with the joy of real serenity.

> *Be thankful in all circumstances, for this is God's will for you who belong to Christ Jesus.—I Thessalonians 5:18 (NLT)*

Mindfully Me

TODAY I WILL:

_____

_____

_____

_____

_____

_____

_____

_____

_____

_____

_____

_____

_____

_____

_____

_____

_____

_____

4.
Timing Is Everything

You are not the only one who feels like life is passing you by. In our world that is overloaded with information, it is easy to begin to think that you have missed your opportunity. But believe me when I tell you that timing is everything. Your clock is unique to you, and you are on schedule. One of the most challenging emotions to live through is the feeling of failure. You haven't failed. You will get there, wherever your "there" is, but not one moment before the right time.

Strawberries are just delicious. Grapes are so delicious. Peaches are totally delicious.

Strawberries usually ripen in four to six weeks. A grapevine can take upwards of three years before it produces edible grapes. A peach tree will produce in about four years, but that depends on so many variables like the climate, if its a dwarf peach tree or a traditional peach tree and if it has enough chill hours. And yet, if you go into the grocery store, each sits in its section on full display in all of its delicious beauty and splendor. They are never jealous of each other, and everyone doesn't purchase everything. People buy what they like.

Everyone will not want what you have to offer. Perceiving that someone has found their way to the display table before you will cause you to experience bitterness. Any fruit that is eaten out of season or prematurely will be bitter. As a matter of fact, the peach that is so juicy and sweet first has to go through a season when it was hard and tasteless. If you are bitter, it's just not time for you…yet! Keep living and waiting. Your day is coming. One day it will be so apparent that it is your turn that people will not be able to get enough of you. In the meantime, keep growing, and enjoying where life has you. If you go too early, no one will want you. Just rest assured that you are being preserved and prepared to be displayed by God and enjoyed by the world - without an ounce of bitterness. The beauty of who you are will be experienced, but timing is everything. Avoid being discouraged today and embrace your connection with The Vine. Your time is coming.

> *There is a right time for everything.—Ecclesiastes 3:1 (TLB)*

Mindfully Me

TODAY I WILL:

Timing Is Everything

Life
Is
Good

5.

Your Struggle Is Your Story

Secrets are overrated. As a child I remember hearing the phrase "what happens in this house, stays in this house." While the sentiment is understandable, unfortunately it enkindled a clandestine culture that advanced a less than healthy and transparent community. The resulting secretive society made many feel as if they were the only person in the world dealing with a challenging state of affairs. But the human race is a family. Our beautiful colors, traditions, and experiences, both good and not so pleasant, help us all grow when we share what we know.

You are not navigating life alone and your perceived profanation is a critical part of your becoming the amazing person that you were designed to be. Someone needs to know your pain, your heartaches, your struggles and your triggers. We all become greater when we can honestly share our journey to wholeness. A misguided public believes that success happens overnight. But the truth is clear. More lessons are learned through struggle and failure than in successes and triumph. While success really feels good, failure is sobering. It is in the sober moments that you are open to life's enlightenment. It is also in those genuine moments that you realize that your most painful defeats weren't actually losses at all, but rather a critical part of your life's story. They made you stronger. They made you focus. They developed your determination. Sharing these narratives with family, friends, coworkers, students and mentees don't make you weak. By owning your moments, all of your moments, you become a real winner. Most superheroes had a weakness, but it never stopped them from becoming the best version of themselves.

It is also critical that you understand this: the person who will be highly anointed with a world changing assignment, will always be someone who has endured great struggle. And when they own it, they know that who they are, and where they are is a result of God's immeasurable grace and undeserved favor which allows them to humbly share their story in the hopes of healing others. Don't be afraid of your story because embracing it allows you to say, like David, that it was good for me to be afflicted.

> *But we have this treasure in jars of clay, to show that the surpassing power belongs to God and not to us.—II Corinthians 4:7 (ESV)*

Mindfully Me

TODAY I WILL:

6.
You Have Everything That You Need

The only person stopping your dreams from becoming reality is you. When you were created, everything that you need to express your peculiar presence and raison d'être was graciously given to you without cost. Furthermore, since your gifts have been freely given, you have a responsibility to develop and distribute them to the world.

So many times we think that we need someone's help, or an opportunity or an open door to accomplish the dreams that we carry in our hearts. But God knows exactly what He's assigned to your hands and has completely equipped you to carry it out with distinction. The only reason that you are having difficulty fulfilling your purpose is this: you are looking around instead of looking within. Being introspective carries with it a degree of difficulty because you cannot deceive yourself about the things within you that you do not like. However, you must take time and look within. It is all part of you. It's what makes you who you are, and your challenge will always be to see beyond what you may not like in order to access the precious endowment that lies inside.

People can encourage you, support you, celebrate you and even write songs about you, but no-one else can bring your precious gift out of you. You must do the hard work of sitting with yourself and making the decision that you will not stop until you release it all. You are the right color, you have the right education, you live in the right neighborhood, and you are the right gender. It is only when you know and truly believe this that you will understand that

You Have Everything That You Need

you unquestionably have everything within you that you need to live your entire life with dignity and purpose right now. Your life will be most comfortable when you are enjoying and embracing you, just as you are, and pulling from the deep well of your substance to make the decisions necessary to finish strong. Close your eyes and connect with the gift that's within, your unique gift from God, and know that it is more than enough.

> *Each of you has been blessed with one of God's many wonderful gifts to be used in the service of others. So use your gift well.—I Peter 4:10 (CEV)*

Mindfully Me

TODAY I WILL:

7.
Quiet Is Refreshing. Quiet Is Good

Our world is filled with so much noise, and every day it seems to get louder and louder. Please don't get it twisted, making a joyful noise to the Lord, singing psalms, hymns and spiritual songs, praying out loud and even fiery preaching is good. And yet, there is an incredible gain to be found in quietude.

When you want to be knowledgeable about what's going on in the world, you'll need to listen to the news on TV or the radio, or scroll through social media. Out of nowhere, your office can get incredibly loud. Sometimes the clangor permeating the surround sound while the children are enjoying their favorite video games can be maddening. Between the screams, songs, sirens and sermons the sounds can actually cause a seemingly unassailable stress. Consequently, the stress can cause insomnia, headaches, body aches, lack of energy and in some cases cancer. Imagine that. The noise is wearing you out. So while good noise in and of itself isn't necessarily bad, quiet is definitely good. And if you want to really tap into a more meaningful life, if you want to live focused, if you want to enjoy supernatural downloads that can transform your personal environment and even the world, you will have to turn off the noise and relish the calm and refreshing that comes in quiet.

It starts with a minute. Don't try to think about it at first. Just try to do it. When you first welcome the stillness, just breathe. Feel your breath. Don't worry about the text or the call that you might be missing. You can handle it later. But in order for you to bring your best creative self into the realm of productivity you must be willing to embrace and enjoy quietude… alone. Silence is actually the place where you can hear clearly. So do it today. Turn off the noise and just hear nothing. Don't be afraid of what you hear. As a matter of fact, you will probably learn some things about yourself that will actually amaze you.

Quiet is a place where you can recharge, revive and renew. Quiet is a major step on your journey to a fulfilling and wholesome existence. It is ok that you have a favorite song or a favorite preacher or that you love watching videos on social media. But if you ever plan to live on a higher plain, the price of your upgrade is simply silence. Quiet is good.

> *It's a good thing to quietly hope, quietly hope for help from God.—Lamentations 3:26 (MSG)*

Mindfully Me

TODAY I WILL:

_____

_____

_____

_____

_____

_____

_____

_____

_____

_____

_____

_____

_____

_____

_____

_____

_____

8.

Learning Lifetime Lessons

Formalized education is extremely necessary in that it teaches you how to learn, and how to develop meaningful interpersonal relationships. But make no mistake about it, learning in no wise ends with a high school diploma, a college degree or the completion of a doctoral program. If you will remain open, life has the ability to teach you the most significant and consequential lessons in every day ordinary moments. Selah.

It is not until you have cried your face off that you appreciate a good laugh. A devastating sickness will cause you to live life to the fullest extent. Not knowing where your next meal is coming from will certainly make you think twice about wasting food in seasons of abundance. And these are lessons that you can only learn by living. However, living is the operative word. You have to live, and that means trying, failing, and trying again. That is when you will learn that failing doesn't mean that you're a failure. Unfortunately, many lives have been wasted because of the fear of trying, the fear of failing or simply being laughed at. Let them laugh. Their laughter, your mistakes or your seemingly endless challenges cannot stop you if make up your mind to win. Yes, in the days of our youth peer pressure and being accepted by the crowd were critical to our existence. But as you get older and mature into your more genuine self, you realize that everyone doesn't have to be your friend and while some people really mean you no harm, they just aren't good for your soul.

The Bible calls it reaping and sowing. The world calls it karma. Whatever you call it, life will teach you that when you are kind without motive, the negativity that consumes so much of our current discourse can't taint your spirit. And while God is definitely gracious, there are some things that we must give an account for before we die. But these are things that we learn along the way. So stay in the school of life and realize that maybe a stop sign or a red light is keeping you from an accident up the road. Maybe a meal dropped on the floor by mistake had poison in it that hadn't been reported yet. Maybe, just maybe, the house you missed or the car you didn't get or the apparent lost love was God protecting you from something that would have devastated you in the future. Just keep living and stay open to learning every single day. What you experience may seem ordinary one day, but it can change your whole perspective on another day.

> *An intelligent heart acquires knowledge, and the ear of the wise seeks knowledge.—Proverbs 18:15 (ESV)*

Mindfully Me

TODAY I WILL:

Learning Lifetime Lessons

WE MUST LAUGH MORE

9.
Right Now Is Good

Tomorrow may never come. That really sounds so cliche, but honestly, where's the lie? It is important to work hard and plan for the future and save for retirement and plan vacations and pay bills and…you get the gist. It's all important, but what is equally important is determining that right now is good.

So may times we miss the joy of today stressing over tomorrow. But just like you will miss your destiny if you're constantly looking back at your history, you do not have the luxury of getting to the end of your life and pressing rewind just to get a little more time. So often we hear people say that life is short, or life is a gift. And yet, we stay angry, hold grudges, live in frustration, walk in bitterness or constantly speak about the good that will happen "some day." Well, beloved, some day is now! Every moment that you are alive is a gift from God that is to be cherished. Even if you are hurting or discouraged, learn how to feel those emotions and then leave them in the previous moment so that you might live in joy.

What if it is your appointed time to die in the next hour. Roughly 60 million people die ever year. That means over 160,000 people die every single day. This is not to bring you down or depress you, but rather to encourage you to balance living and planning. Make certain that you laugh every day. Promise yourself that you will do something every single day for you that makes you happy. Tomorrow will be good if you get there, but since you already have today, make it good. Jesus did not die for you to be unhappy. He wants you to have a better life than you could have ever dreamed. So please do what He wants…live! You don't have to offend anyone or be wild and crazy to prove that you're living your best life. Just make sure that at the end of every single day you can say "it was good." The issues of tomorrow will be there if you get there.

> *Who of you by worrying can add a single hour to his life?—Matthew 6:7 (BSB)*

Mindfully Me

TODAY I WILL:

_____

_____

_____

_____

_____

_____

_____

_____

_____

_____

_____

_____

_____

_____

_____

10.
Peace...The Perfect Place

It is absolutely possible to have the best and the finest of every material thing imaginable and be miserable. You can be a creative genius with infinite possibilities and be in bondage to resentment and envy. There are actually people who contend for the faith with purposeful passion and live in secret doubt.

Peace that passes understanding comes when you do the difficult work of thinking differently about what happens in your life. So many times we ask the question "why is this happening to me," when the better question is "why is this happening *for* me?" We live in frustration because of what hasn't worked instead of celebrating what has worked. We mark the successes of our friends and family and wonder if we will ever have a turn. Don't worry, you will have a turn, but only after you have learned how to ignore some of the reoccurring thoughts and attitudes that block your peace.

Peace is the perfect place because genuine love and healthy living automatically flow when you're at peace. That means you will have to chose not to fight some battles and abandon the desire to win everything all of the time. Negativity cannot be an option if you really desire perfect peace. Unfortunately, that means that there are some family members, coworkers, neighbors and maybe even friends who you will have to give breathing room so that they too may live in peace. That's not cancel culture as much as it is being conscientious.

Possessions, accomplishments and people mean absolutely nothing when you don't have peace. If, however, you have peace, you will never be bitter or angry when you have to maintain, renew or nurture any of them.

> *He will keep in perfect peace all those who trust in Him, whose thoughts turn often to the Lord.—Isaiah 26:3 (TLB)*

Mindfully Me

TODAY I WILL:

11.
Exhale...Again!

Life throws a lot at you. Every single day. Consequently, just getting from one day to the next can be breath taking. The phrase "if it ain't one thing, it's another" rings true in your mind. Sickness. Bills. Disappointment. Heartache. Pain. Confusion. No energy. No sleep. No money. No friends. No relief in sight. And all of this causes you to freeze because you don't want to go off or explode. You feel if one more thing happens, you will certainly double detonate!

Exhale friend.

God breathed into humankind to give us life. Every time you inhale, you are literally receiving a gift from God. However, His desire is that you give to the world what He has invested into you. Every time you exhale, you are actually indicating that you are open to receive more and share more. True gratefulness is appreciating every single breath and willingly releasing your life for God's purpose, knowing that He will always supply your need…your breath.

So when it feels like it's too much, and it will, just exhale. Exhaling is releasing. When you pass away, you will be emptied of breath. While you are alive, trust the giver of life and release the old and expect the blessing that comes with each new breath. Relax your shoulders, release the tension, and rest in the loving arms of God and know that everything is going to be alright - but it all starts with one simple exercise. Exhale…again! Stay ready for the new blessings. Stay open to releasing the past. And when it resurfaces, let it go. Exhale…again! Selah.

Exhale…Again!

When you control your breathing, you control your moments. The next moment is not promised to you, so make this one superior. As long as you're breathing, you have life, and as long as you're alive, there is still hope.

Exhale…again!

> *The Spirit of God hath made me, and the breath of the Almighty hath given me life.—Job 33:4 (KJV)*

Mindfully Me

TODAY I WILL:

_____
_____
_____
_____
_____
_____
_____
_____
_____
_____
_____
_____
_____
_____
_____
_____
_____
_____
_____

12.

Watch Words.
Learn Words.

Words have power. That's why we enjoy people who encourage or inspire us with their words. That is also why we avoid people who incessantly complain, belittle and criticize. The words that you speak or allow someone to speak over you will directly impact your life in more ways than you think.

A parent who tells a child that they can be whatever they want to be pushes that child, simply by those words to achieve and often overachieve in their lifetime. There is a confidence that is built into a child who is celebrated.

However, a child who is called stupid or dumb actually believes that and will often live a frustrated life with low self-esteem and rage. As both of these children become adults, they will imitate and replicate the words that formed their world. Hence, one will be extremely positive and encourage others in the same way, while the other is constantly fighting bitterness and a subtle rage because they were mishandled as a child.

The good news is that you really have the power to wipe the slate clean, erase all of the negativity that was deposited into your spirit, and start anew. That means, however, that you will have to watch your words. The inclination to agree with those respected persons from your formative years is enormous. But this is your life. This is your journey. And this is your time to take back your power and rework, remake and remodel your life into what you know it can be. Be your own life coach and disregard the words that hurt and learn new words. Affirm yourself. Speak so clearly to your spirit that the pain of the old words no longer penetrate your existence.

When you inaugurate mastering unfamiliar locutions, then every moribund moment will become a halcyon day. You will literally honor the beauty of your being. God does…why shouldn't you?

> *Kind words are like honey, sweet to the soul and healthy for the body.— Proverbs 18:24 (NLT)*

Mindfully Me

TODAY I WILL:

Watch Words. Learn Words.

You Are Going To Be OK!

13.

Shut Off Default Mode

The default mode is that pesky little inner voice that keeps you embarrassed about or in bondage to your past. It reminds you of your mistakes and your failures. It makes you worry and fear about tomorrow. It makes you count your money five times a day, even when you haven't spent any money at all. It will cause you to call yourself negative names when no one is around. Shut it off!

While the default mode can assist you in making good choices, if you continue to live in the past and fret about the future, then you will always miss the beauty of today. You cannot change the past. You can absolutely do your best to do better, but what is done is done. There is no do-over of yesterday. No, my friend, there is no such thing as a time machine. It's over. Could you have done some things differently? Probably. But God's incredible mercy is so amazing that it actually waits for you to wake up each day so that it can shower you with a fresh supply. Don't allow the default mode to cause you to miss the wonder of today, while you shed tears over a yesterday that you cannot change. Be a good steward of this moment. That also means, however, that you cannot overwhelm yourself with the unknown. It generally results in fear, and fear will always leave you frozen. You lose sleep. You overthink everything. You embrace conspiracies, and you will eventually make your own self sick, literally and figuratively.

Americans are overworked and most of them are underpaid. This causes many to try to "stay on their grind" or "keep up with the Jones'" and unfortunately, this has caused many people to work their whole lives only to die right after they retire. Mix it up. Work some. Play some. Save some. Spend some. Dance some. Sit some. Read some. Write some. But in the midst of it all, never forget that God's plan for your life is good. If you can only learn to flow with it, your life will be greater than you ever imagined. Do it today. Don't announce it. Don't post it. But make a conscious decision to trust that everything that you need for today will be attracted to you today. And then watch God work.

You have the finger to flip the on/off button in either direction.

> *This is the day that the Lord has made; let us rejoice and be glad in it.—Psalm 118:24 (ESV)*

Mindfully Me

TODAY I WILL:

_____

_____

_____

_____

_____

_____

_____

_____

_____

_____

_____

_____

_____

_____

_____

_____

_____

14.

Worry Is Sin

It is certain that life is uncertain. Everyone has to maneuver unexpected opposition at some time or another. There is no way around it. Graveyards are filled with boxes that house bones of people who were millionaires, wielded great power, developed medicines, and who since have entered the history books. No amount of creativity or brute strength can keep you out of the graveyard. When you die, you will be dead for a long time. Therefore, it becomes imperative that you live and enjoy each day without worrying.

When you know that God loves you, there is no need to worry about anything. Everything may not work out the way that you want, but it will be okay. You must believe that with every fiber of your being. Worry is in effect the expectation of an unfavorable outcome before it happens. It is in essence having faith in the negative. Just like a frown is an upside-down smile, worry is inverted faith. It is virtually impossible to believe God and worry. You must pick one. Faith is critical to please God. If that is true, then it stands to reason that worry is sin. Not only is it sin, but it causes anxiety and actual measurable pain in your body. Imagine that! You could start feeling better today if, and only if, you would release the inclination to worry.

Worrying doesn't make it better. Worrying doesn't fix anything. Worrying doesn't develop ideas. Worrying doesn't give rise to dreams. Worrying doesn't affect happiness. In all honesty, worry is a waste of your time, energy and thoughts. Repossess your time. Recover your energy. Reclaim your thoughts. You have too much life to live and big ideas to manifest. You will win, and if you don't win, you will learn valuable lessons that are necessary for the next place on your pilgrimage.

Please don't misspend your life expecting bad things to happen. God really does have an amazing master plan with your name on it. However, you will not experience the panoply of your tailor-made blessings if you worry.

> *Therefore I tell you, do not worry about your life, what you will eat or drink; or about your body, what you will wear. Is not life more than food, and the body more than clothes?—Matthew 6:25 (NIV)*

Mindfully Me

TODAY I WILL:

15.

Perceive Temporary and Terminal

More often than not, the challenging seasons of your life are temporary. And yet, so many give up in a trial that was originally permitted to teach, not terminate. To be spiritual, one must have the ability to see things that do not exist and then transition them from the realm of the unseen into the here and now. However, that takes laser focus and unfeigned strength of will.

Loving God does not mean everyone will love you or even be your friend. Doing good to others doesn't mean that you will have only good days. You can smile at everyone you meet every day, all day, but that does not guarantee that people who smile in your face won't stab you in the back. However, you can rest assured that the pain that you feel in those instances is not forever. Great storms produce great people. Tornadoes are deadly, but if you are deeply rooted, you will live to see peace in the middle of that same lethal twister. You will still have to suffer through the back half of the tornado, but if you lived through the beginning, you can certainly make it through the second half. It has been said that everyone is either in a storm, coming out of a storm, or going into a storm. You have to perceive what is temporary. Otherwise, you will misdiagnose your moment.

There are some situations that must die. They are no good for us. Their season is over, and in many cases, they were never meant to be in the first place. Oh yes, we have welcomed some affairs that were never meant to ever exist. But God is so kind and His love is so big, that He will wait for us to extinguish the terminal.

Perceive Temporary And Terminal

There is something so incredibly powerful that is waiting in the tomorrow of every survivor. The challenge will always be recognizing the difference between the seasons of "this too will pass" and "it is done." When you master that, you will be unstoppable.

> *These troubles and sufferings of ours are, after all, quite small and won't last very long. Yet this short time of distress will result in God's richest blessing upon us forever and ever.—II Corinthians 4:17 (TLB)*

Mindfully Me

TODAY I WILL:

16.
It's Only A Test

Isn't it funny that when we were in school we all knew that the teacher was silent during the test, but it wasn't until we became adults and lived through tests that we realized what that exercise really meant. Well, here's the plot twist. While you are living through the test, your adversary peeked into your future and saw the answer. He knows that you're going to win. He knows that you are the head and not the tail. He knows that you are more than a conqueror. And he is currently launching an all-out attack on your destiny.

You must never forget that you are God's child. And while that is great for you, the devil is jealous of you. Every time he sees you, he is reminded of what he's lost. His jealousy and hatred for you causes him to incessantly throw darts and dig ditches to trip you up. Please don't lose heart beloved. It is only a test, and you're going to pass with flying colors. You have been chosen for this season and this time. While you are living in this moment, the devil is not fighting who you are, he is trying to destroy the ensuing, mature you, the you who is going to change the world for good. Hell is afraid of your future. This particular test has nothing to do with sin. It is all about your destiny. So while you are in the process of maturing into what you can't see just yet, never forget that people who aren't going *through* anything are usually the people who aren't going anywhere. The operative word is through. You are not stuck. If the Children of Israel were not on their way to their wealthy place, they would not have had to traverse through hell and high water. Israel's destiny, abundance, and promise was secure, but the adversary had to do everything possible to trick them into giving up before they arrived in their predetermined location.

There is nothing that can stop you from getting there. There is no fire hot enough, there is no river deep enough, there is no mountain high enough, there is heartache painful enough, there is no depression dark enough, there is no problem hard enough to stop you from getting there. This might be a seriously rough patch, but it is only a test. Don't worry, you're an A+ student.

> *Thou hast caused me to ride over our heads; we went through fire and through water: but though broughtest us out into a wealthy place.— Psalm 66:12 (KJV)*

Mindfully Me

TODAY I WILL:

It's Only A Test

Often In Life You Will Lose A Few Battles, But That Doesn't Mean You'll Lose The War!

FIGHT ON SOLDIER!

17.

Tears Legitimize You

A wise woman by the name of Erdice Natalie Scott once told me that your tears simply mean that you are full of joy or pain and when you cry, you release the joy or the pain and make room for what's next. What an amazing perspective to have about something that we all experience - tears, joy and pain.

In reality, all that she was saying is that tears simply mean you are alive, and as long as you are alive, you can have hope. Welcome the hope that pain won't last forever, and that joy has purpose. Frustration, anger, and bitterness are all released when you allow yourself to cry. The static will keep you going in circles if you don't cry.

Tears legitimize you. They mean that you love. They mean that you hurt. They mean that you have feelings. They mean that you care. They mean that you have dreams. They mean that you made plans. They mean that people matter. They mean that issues matter. They mean that you have goals. They mean that you have aspirations. They mean that your life matters. They mean that everything concerning you matters. Your tears mean that you exist. Fallen exanimate people don't cry.

Furthermore, God keeps track of every single one of your tears and has recorded each one of them in a book. Your pain is not in vain. You should always know that God is for you. He sees, He knows and He cares.

Finally, because there is a season and a time to every purpose under the heaven, your tears have a purpose. Sometimes the dark nights of the soul seem like an unending eternity, but tears are a prerequisite for joy. Never forget it.

Tears Legitimize You

You're alive and as long as you're alive, . Joy IS coming because every promise from God is true.

> *There is hope only for the living. "It is better to be a live dog than a dead lion!"—Ecclesiastes 9:4 (TLB)*

Mindfully Me

TODAY I WILL:

_____

_____

_____

_____

_____

_____

_____

_____

_____

_____

_____

_____

_____

_____

_____

_____

_____

18.
Prayer Really Works

Prayer and supplication with thanksgiving will always bring you peace. If you really want genuine peace in your life, however, waiting until you are in an emergency situation and running into the hospital chapel like they do on the soap operas (at least that's the way it was years ago) may not afford you the peace necessary for daily living.

If you see prayer as an inconvenient exercise early in the morning or due to some mandate from a spiritual leader, you have already missed the point. Rest assured that every great world changer or pensive person has made prayer a routine practice. Occasionally the time spent in prayer is longer than others. In many seasons, there is no response to the prayers offered. But they continue in prayer because it has a centering effect. As a matter of fact, scientists have proven that regular prayer reduces stress, calms anxiety and helps people maintain a proper perspective in relation to life's strife filled encounters.

Though often loud and verbose, prayer can be quite quiet and simple. Fancy words don't impress God. Sincerity, on the other hand, will capture God's attention every time. If the truth is told, there are some things said in prayer that we really don't want anyone else to hear. God is, however, always pleased when we share them with Him, even when the words aren't uttered or given sound. The meditations of your heart are understood when appropriate words seem to fail you.

Additionally, genuine prayer always incorporates thanksgiving. When you refuse to solely look at the negative, but passionately and purposefully live in thankfulness, you will experience a deep tranquility and quietude that cannot be measured. God loves it when we ask of Him, because it means that we are humbly submitting to His power, will and ability. Think about how you feel when someone says "thank you." It's amazing what those two little words can do. They make the administrator work overtime. They make the teacher work harder. They make the pastor study fervently. They make the child help out around the house willingly. So imagine how God feels when you abide in thankfulness. Everyone, yes everyone, has something to complain about. But thank you makes room for more peace, blessings, favor, love and real happiness. Prayer really works, but you have to keep praying no matter what.

> *Pray without ceasing.*
> *—I Thessalonians 5:17 (KJV)*

Mindfully Me

TODAY I WILL:

19.
Miracles Still Happen

How incredible is it to know that we are constantly moving, even when we are sitting still. The gift of gravity keeps you firmly on a planet that is moving somewhere in the neighborhood of 1,000 miles per hour. Let that sink in. If God didn't want to bless you with incredible miracles, the world would just stop - right now, and then we would all go flying out into space.

You are here because there is a good plan for your life, and it includes big, bold and exciting miracles every single day. Unfortunately, the American psyche has made us think that miracles = money. Regrettably, money cannot buy you everything. Sure, money can do a lot of good. After all, according to Ecclesiastes 10:19, money makes the world go round. But don't be fooled. There are very wealthy people who have loads of money, but can't enjoy it because they are in a coma or they are a quadriplegic. Money can buy you a beautiful mansion, but it can't buy you a home filled with love and acceptance.

Miracles are those divine interventions into the affairs of mere men that cause joy and are most welcomed, but inexplicable. A miracle is when the doctor "calls the family in" to give bad news, only to find a few hours later that the doctor was wrong. A miracle is when someone crashes into you, the car turns over 5 times and ends up facing the wrong way on the other side of the road - and you walk away without a scratch. A miracle is when you create something, and nothing happens for a long, long time and then out of nowhere your creativity blesses someone who subsequently changes the trajectory of your life.

Miracles Still Happen

Miracles still happen. You may not see it or feel it right now, but there is a miracle heading your way. You wouldn't have appreciated this incredible breakthrough that is assigned to your life last year. It's all coming together, but you must keep believing. How cool is it to know that you are constantly moving and yet, a miracle is about to chase you down! Your anxiety is about to be traded for something that you never expected if you stay open to the possibility of miracles. God wants to do things in your life far beyond what you can imagine or perceive, but your faith in Him must be secure. It doesn't have to be big, but it must be secure.

> *Behold, I am the Lord, the God of all flesh: is there anything too hard for me?—Jeremiah 32:27 (KJV)*

Mindfully Me

TODAY I WILL:

_____

_____

_____

_____

_____

_____

_____

_____

_____

_____

_____

_____

_____

_____

_____

_____

_____

20.

Keep Feeling This Moment

You can be overwhelmed with your issues or you can be overjoyed that you are alive. The choice is yours. It's not an easy choice. You must work on it over and over and over. But it is attainable. Worry and fear will nag you at every turn. You literally have to make the decision that you will live in this moment.

The challenge with feeling this moment is that sometimes you will feel pain. Often you will feel numb. You may even feel disgusted. The key is learning how to feel the moment without allowing the moment to control or smother you. Being fully present is not about being philosophical or spooky, but rather appreciative that you have the gift of inhaling and exhaling without the assistance of a machine. It's about knowing that life will happen, but you don't have to be stressed out about anything… ever. Being present means trusting that the joy, sadness, apprehension, boredom and serenity all play into your ultimate goal of being at peace. It's knowing that you don't have to retaliate or get revenge or scheme because your times are in God's hands.

You have so much to celebrate, even if the present space that you are occupying is weird or uncomfortable. You have mastered the art of waking up every day. Why not take advantage of the precious gift of this day and allow yourself to enjoy what others complain about? There is a very powerful lesson to be learned in right now. It is necessary for your peace tomorrow. Don't let this moment pass you by. Try to distance yourself from the notion that your perceived perfection is the way it has to be. In doing so, you can save yourself a great deal of unnecessary suffering. Feel this moment because honestly, it's all that you really have. So live it. Enjoy it. Most of all, love it. It just may be your last moment.

> *How do you know what is going to happen tomorrow? For the length of your lives is as uncertain as the morning fog – now you see it; soon it is gone.—James 4:14 (TLB)*

Mindfully Me

TODAY I WILL:

Keep Feeling This Moment

IT'S NOT SELFISH TO TAKE CARE OF *You!*

21.

Sitting With The Sovereign

Please reject the notion that if you are not grinding 24/7 that your life doesn't matter or you won't be successful. A few years ago, there was a relatively popular expression that said "have a seat." While laziness is never an option, there is so much more to a meaningful existence than working and toiling and laboring until you die.

There is more than one way to skin a cat. There is more than one way to be successful. There is more than one way to obtain the anointing. Elisha would not let Elijah out of his sight. Elisha pursued Elijah's anointing. After Saul's disobedience, Samuel sought out Jesse's son David because God had chosen him. David had a chosen anointing. Then there is a special anointing for people who have not obtained a pursued anointing, nor do they enjoy a chosen anointing. This is the anointing that is for people who love righteousness. They don't have a spiritual father who calls them exceptional. They don't have any particular skill like singing or preaching or playing an instrument that solidifies their position among the anointed. They don't have a great name or significant familial status. They don't have colossal wealth that was earned or inherited. They don't have noteworthy degrees after their names. They just love righteousness. They love being in God's presence and doing whatever His word says is right. Sure, they have questions, but the written and spoken Word of God is their final authority.

There are so many situations that can be settled when you just sit with The Sovereign. Wisdom will overtake your life if you listen to the instructions and love them, even when they cut to the core. There is a glory that will overshadow you if you allow God's word to daily breathe life into your spirit. This phrase is not shared in a rude or disrespectful way, but have a seat. When you sit with The Sovereign, you can expect great solace and comfort. You can also expect unspeakable joy and peace that will give you security and direction in your daily choices. Take a rest and open your ears to The Sovereign God who has everything under control. If you do what you hear, you will be successful.

> *You have loved righteousness and hated lawlessness; this is why God, your God, has anointed you with the oil of joy beyond your companions.— Hebrews 1:9 (CSB)*

Mindfully Me

TODAY I WILL:

22.
That Is Their Choice

Periodically someone who means the world to you will do something that makes you cry, makes you concerned, or maybe even feel troubled. From time to time, those feelings turn to worry that causes you to be super stressed. After all, you love them and they're important to you, right? But isn't it funny how they continue living their best life while you're in search of pain meds for your headache because of their actions.

People are going to do what they want to do. That is not bad, that is their choice. You can't make anyone love you. You can't make anyone treat you right. That is their choice. You can, however, decide that you are the arbiter of your peace. Think about it. As children, our parents often told us things that we shouldn't do - and we did them anyway. It's because there is something in us that needs to explore and experience the world in our own way and in our own time. You will end up having a stroke attempting to control another human being. On the other hand, you will taste the sweet fruit of calm when you allow people to live their own lives, whether it be to their detriment or their advantage.

Actually, when we work overtime to restrict the freedoms of another human being, we run the risk of functioning as a judge. Of course, your intentions are good or even for their good. But people must be allowed to learn, live, grow and become as they choose. You will experience a significant level of tranquility when you let them live. It doesn't mean that you don't care, nor does it mean that your love has decreased. It does, however, mean that you have come to terms with the fact that in many cases, it is simply more prudent to leave them in hands of The Lord. The same God who kept you when someone was praying for you will keep them as you pray for them. But just as your life is yours to live, it is ok for them to have dreams, desires, plans, proclivities, activities and absorptions that don't jive with your judgement. Believe in God and believe in the power of your prayers and if you release them to be free, you will also enjoy freedom.

> *If the Son therefore shall make you free, ye shall be free indeed.—John 8:36 (KJV)*

Mindfully Me

TODAY I WILL:

23.
Destruction and Construction

Have you been feeling like everything is crumbling around you? Your family is out of control. Many of your friends have walked away. Your money is funny, change is strange and your credit won't get it. Before you seek an audience with God for your perceived abandonment issues, maybe something else is going on.

Could it be that God is allowing the destruction before the construction of the new and improved you? What if there are some cracks in your foundation that would not be able to handle the weightiness of the mature you? It is a known fact that before you erect up, you must dig down deep in order to build a firm foundation. And oddly enough, the foundation, something that is critical to the strength and maintenance of the building, is virtually invisible. Don't misdiagnose the destruction process. It is not the end. It is the commencement of your new beginning. In the meantime, read books, ask questions, keep a journal, and do whatever is possible to expand your thinking about where it is you ultimately desire to go. Develop a diet for new knowledge and try to learn or rehearse something, no matter how small, every single day.

You are in the process of becoming. Stay open to the lessons that you learn during this time of loss. If you can just hold on for a little while longer, everyone is going to see your substance, character and usefulness. They will know that you spent time with God. They will also know that you have been chosen for your moment. However, please be aware of the change orders. Change orders are new expenses that occur during construction that you were not aware of when you started the project. If you knew what it was going to cost you to reach your full maturity, your destiny, you would have given up a long time ago. Many wouldn't even start. That is why information is revealed as you go. That is why you must daily trust God and know that just because you're uncomfortable, it does not mean that the goal is unattainable. You would be suspicious of any structure that commenced construction on Thursday and opened for business on Friday. There is no need to agonize in the destruction. After you survive your construction, you will not be moved.

> *...to equip the saints for the work of ministry, for building up the Body of Christ...to mature manhood.— Ephesians 4:12-13 (ESV)*

Mindfully Me

TODAY I WILL:

24.

Music Manifests Miracles

Never ever forget that you have a God given right to sing off key, as loud as you'd like. Of course that's not the case if you're in the choir, but it is absolutely true everywhere else. (Please don't try this in a court of law or in an office setting that expects quiet, but you understand the point.)

Just as quiet can bring healing, music, good music, will change your mood in an incredible way. David played the lyre and ministered to Saul's spirit. Music is therapeutic. It can help you manage anxiety and it has been known to alleviate pain. The right song will diminish your level of stress and bring comfort to a broken, troubled or wounded heart. Music can take the edge off of your work out and make it so much more enjoyable. Music is good for your soul.

Music, in and of itself, isn't right or wrong. Different songs work for different moments. You may like music from your youth or the classics that stand the test of time. Sometimes a screaming song will energize you just as a soft one can bring you to tears. You might like Ludwig Van Beethoven, The Beatles, Whitney Houston, James Cleveland or Louis Armstrong. Like who you like for whatever moment you're in. Make a playlist for specific moods like rainy day music, or music to clean the house, or music for a drive on a sunny day - and then let it work its wonder.

Before you argue, play a few of your favorite songs. Before a stressful meeting, sing a song that lifts you. Before you make a major decision, slow down, listen to that song again and then expect the miracle that only music can manifest.

Music Manifests Miracles

It really works. And the best part is that you can put on your headphones and escape and travel to your happy place without anyone's permission. Do yourself a favor and get lost in some music, some good music. It will catapult you into your place of miracles, and even if some songs make you cry, you also know some that will always make you smile. So go have another listen, or you can just sing - off key if you'd like. Your music will manifest your miracle.

> *Talk with each other much about the Lord, quoting psalms and hymns and singing sacred songs, making music in your hearts to the Lord.— Ephesians 5:19 (TLB)*

Mindfully Me

TODAY I WILL:

Music Manifests Miracles

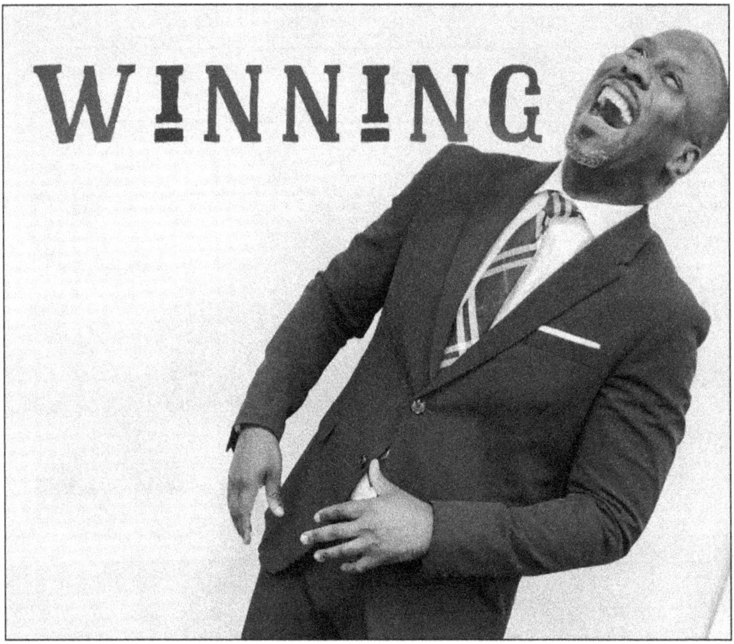
WINNING

25.
Sacrifice Superficial Subjects

Everything doesn't matter. Everything cannot be important to you. Unfortunately, too much of what we have deemed as significant is really superficial. You must determine for your life, for your world, the true and central subjects.

A subject can be defined as a train of thought, a writing, a theme or a class that one studies. There are very few of us who can master everything. Generally we tend to shine in one particular area or another. Many can stand out in a few. But it is unusually rare that someone is an expert in everything. Your serenity depends on you being willing to release the needless things and focus well on the principle things. It doesn't mean that you can't be entertained by them or even interested in them, but real wisdom motivates you to give your best energy to the key undertakings. No one else can choose them for you. Furthermore, you will never have genuine contentment when waste your time and energy copying others. At best you will be an understudy or a substitute, but never the best version of yourself.

A subject can also be defined as a person. Unfortunately, far too often we allow superficial subjects to overstay their appointed time in our lives. Sometimes it is loneliness, lack of self-esteem, or just habit that we allow them to continue past their designated expiration date in our existence. You know it's over. You don't hate them, but you feel awkward when they come around. You sigh and roll your eyes when you see their number on your caller ID. Beloved, without being negative, unpleasant or unkind

Sacrifice Superficial Subjects

you must sacrifice those subjects. You know it and they already feel it. Why do you keep waiting to pull the plug on a relationship that is on life support? Your soul is waiting for you to make the move and make the sacrifice. Your security cannot be connected to the superficial. You cannot have a treaty where there should be a termination.

If you will make the often difficult and uncomfortable resolution to sacrifice every superficial subject, you will find that God's pronouncement of peace for your life will be sweeter than honey.

> *Brethren, I count not myself to have apprehended: but this one thing I do, forgetting those things which are behind, and reaching forth unto those things which are before, I press toward the mark for the prize of the high calling of God in Christ Jesus.—Philippians 3:13-14 (KJV)*

Mindfully Me

TODAY I WILL:

26.
It Took A Long Time...

There is a season for everything, and a time for every purpose. Time. Every purpose takes time, time and more time. In a world where most people under 20 have never heard of a typewriter or a rotary dial phone, time has a different meaning than it did 100 years ago.

Before music streaming, you had to wait for a record to come out and hope that your local record store had the recording that you wanted. Before incessant texts, we had emails and people had to wait until you logged on to your computer to respond. Before emails, we had faxes and you had to wait for people to go

Mindfully Me

to the office. Before faxes, we had letters and you had to wait for the postal service. Before direct deposit at midnight of payday, you had to go to work to get your check. Before food delivery services, we had to go to the grocery store. Before microwave ovens, or ovens, we had to start a fire. Before $200 a month cable bills, we had 3 free stations. Everything is faster now and when you get accustomed to things happening quickly, you expect everything to happen fast. However, there are some things that just take time. School takes time. No matter how hard you try, you can't make your birthday come any quicker than it did last year.

It took a long time for you to get to where you are. You weren't born yesterday. And wherever you are going will require that even more time passes. Sure, there are times when God will seemingly speed up the process, and give you an "immediately" miracle, however, that is usually because there is a specific purpose. So since it took time and it's going to take time, enjoy this time. This day. This hour. This minute.

This second. Maybe you can't eat the whole bag of potato chips, but you can have one. Maybe you can't take the six month cruise around the world, but you can take a weekend excursion. Please enjoy every second of your life because in a little while they will be no more.

Finally, when you feel stuck, hopeless or discouraged, reflect on all of the time that it has taken for you to get here. Remind yourself of your victories. Reminisce on the good friends that made you laugh. Reflect on the moments when you won. And then neatly tuck it away to enjoy later, and get back to enjoying this moment, resting assured that if you made it through before, you will make it through again.

> *...please don't squander one bit of this marvelous life God has given us. God reminds us, I heard your call in the nick of time; The day you needed me, I was there to help.*
> *—II Corinthians 6:1-2 (MSG)*

Mindfully Me

TODAY I WILL:

_____

_____

_____

_____

_____

_____

_____

_____

_____

_____

_____

_____

_____

_____

_____

_____

27.
ALL MEANS ALL

Have you ever wondered why you didn't lose it? Have you ever tried to figure out why other people caught a case when you didn't? Or have you ever wondered why you caught the case, but the process didn't destroy you? We all know people who just can't seem to get it together. But it's different for you. You love God and that means despite how you might be feeling, you know it's all going to work out in the end.

2020 was a year for the history books. The pandemic gave a new meaning to "a crazy year." There was heartbreaking death, loss, unheard of sickness and daily confusion. Let's just face it, there was a fear that had many people wondering if they were coming or going. Countless congregations lost leaders. So many families lost their provider. Innumerable entrepreneurs lost their businesses. And interestingly enough, God in His infinite wisdom still allowed us to have some good days. When we were able to smile, it felt really good. But honestly, the lows felt extra low. It felt as if when we laughed, we really laughed hard, but when we cried, we cried much harder than we laughed. True to form, God gave you great victories, but the adversary antagonized you to no end.

Relax beloved. Even though it has felt like no sooner than you get out of a trial, here comes a tribulation, you must celebrate the fact that you are still here. Selah. Jesus made it unequivocally clear that as long as you are in the world, you will have tribulation. But when you walk with Him, and talk with Him and learn of Him and embrace His yoke, you will have peace. Instead of magnifying the problem, seek to understand its purpose. Most of the medicine in the store now is loaded with sugar and honey. There was a time, however, when medicine had such a disgusting taste that you didn't want to take it. But it made you better. The temporary inconvenience of the aftertaste couldn't compare to how you would feel when you were really better.

Be strong and take heart. It may not all make sense. It certainly may not work the way you'd like. It more than likely won't feel good. But you love God, so in the final analysis it will be good. Exhale again and start expecting the God who gives good gifts to grace you with the energy necessary to persevere.

> *Meanwhile, the moment we get tired in the waiting, God's Spirit is right alongside helping us along…That's why we can be so sure that every detail in our lives of love for God is worked into something good.—Romans 8:26-28 (MSG)*

Mindfully Me

TODAY I WILL:

_____

_____

_____

_____

_____

_____

_____

_____

_____

_____

_____

_____

_____

_____

_____

_____

_____

_____

28.
BEING BENEVOLENT BLESSES

THE EMOTIONAL, PHYSICAL AND SPIRItual exhaustion that you face from the daily challenges surrounding mere survival will often impel you to curl up in the fetal position, close your eyes really tightly and pray for the pain to cease. Usually that's not enough. Unfortunately, more often than not, we pick up habits that really aren't good for us. And we know that they aren't good, but the relief from the incessant agony almost makes it seem worth the habit.

Before you give in to the practice of your proclivity, consider sharing a kind word, thought or deed, without expecting anything in return. Now this one is truly a challenge. Everyone can be kind to people who love them, support them or who are always rooting for them. But how you treat people who will never have the ability to bless you back speaks volumes about your character. Being kind is an act of love, and let's face it, when people are thoughtful and caring, it can actually change your entire mood. Just like a crazy text or call can push you off the deep end, a kind-hearted considerate act can cause unexpected elation.

One of the reasons that it is important to be altruistic with strangers is because you can't manipulate them in the future by reminding them what you did for them. When you are selfless with strangers, you make a deposit with God, and God always takes care of those who bless His children. It is also important to be kind and loving with the people you know. It will lift your spirit when you see how you were able to brighten their day. But when you do any act of kindness, never expect anything in return. Do it because it's right. Do it because it's good. Do it because God loves it. Do it not only because you will lift someone's spirit, but because being benevolent blesses you too. God keeps good records and pays you back better than any mere human being ever could.

Your kindness will often be misunderstood. That's why it is best to do it in secret and expect nothing. Don't talk about it. You will often be misunderstood when caring for another soul. Don't try to explain it. Don't keep a record. Don't cry about it. Like the stock market that generally takes years to give you a return, if you keep making investments into others, there will come a day when you are so abundantly blessed, you will know it was only because being benevolent became your lifestyle.

> *Love one another with brotherly affection. Outdo one another in showing honor…Rejoice in hope, be patient in tribulation, be constant in prayer. Contribute to the needs of the saints and seek to show hospitality.—Romans 12:10,12-13 (ESV)*

Mindfully Me

TODAY I WILL:

Being Benevolent Blesses

PROMOTION IS ONLY FOR PEOPLE WHO PRESS THROUGH PROCESS

29.
Everything Wasn't A Lie

When you heard what they said about you, you spiraled into a melancholy that affected your entire world. Some moments you felt anger. Sometimes it was rage. When a trusted confidant releases information that you entrusted to them from a place of perceived deep friendship, it can be devastating. That friend told a friend and their friend told a friend and you lie in your bed in a numbness fueled by embarrassment and disbelief.

The problem that you are dealing with is simple. It didn't happen quite like they said, but everything wasn't a lie. So what do you say? Who can you trust? Do you take to social media to try to fix the situation? Do you call your friend and ask why they would betray you? Do you leave town? Embarrassment and pain will make you do some crazy things, often things that aren't necessary.

When we commence with the fact that everything that they said was not a lie, you are setting yourself up to have victory in a trial. Jesus did not come into the world to suffer betrayal, abuse, mistreatment and then get nailed to a cross for perfect people. Read that again. No one is perfect. Today is the day that you must learn the value in knowing that truth, honesty and candor will make you free. My mother used to say that "people don't have a heaven or hell to put you in." Jesus died for it before you did it. You will enjoy unprecedented calm when you live your life to please God and not people. People move the goal posts. People change. And most importantly, people aren't God. No, you don't want to bring reproach upon the Body of Christ, but many prospective converts stay away from the Kingdom of God because of incessant, blatant hypocrisy. Jesus is the way, the truth and the life. Let your comfort be in The Truth. That may mean that you will have a shorter Christmas list, but you will have a greater life of authenticity. God loves truth, so be what God loves. The lies don't matter as much as you think they do. They reveal important lessons about alliances and friendship choices. But ultimately truth, even the painful truth about yourself will set you apart to become genuine. Genuine is good.

> *Lying lips are an abomination to the Lord, but those who deal truthfully are His delight.—Proverbs 12:22 (NKJV)*

TODAY I WILL:

_____
_____
_____
_____
_____
_____
_____
_____
_____
_____
_____
_____
_____
_____
_____
_____
_____
_____

30.
Go For Broke

You only have one chance at this life. Please don't waste it with regret, sadness, depression, uncertainty, negative thinking or overthinking. God has a magnificent plan for you. But it is true that things that you work for, suffer for or wait for are so much more meaningful than so called overnight successes. The lessons learned in the struggle last for a lifetime. The strength gained in the passing of time is indestructible.

But if you are going to make it, you're going to have to give it all you have and go for broke. The tests, trials, tears and tragedies that you face are all part of your incredible uniqueness. They make your story original. In this day and age, it is becoming easier and easier to spot the spurious. So make every experience count. Embrace the challenges. Accept the dare. Live your life. The brokenness, discouragement and even your apprehensions all have a purpose. It is a waste of time to succumb to a pessimistic vantage point. Learn and grow from the incidents, but please don't park in the pain that was only permitted for pause.

You are responsible for living your life and no-one else can do it for you. Give it all that you have. When you refuse to be defeated, you keep moving towards God's intended goal for your course of life. Listen, you're going to get there - wherever there is. Enjoy the trip. You must become comfortable allowing some things to simply roll off your back. Pick your battles carefully. Do you want to be right or do you want to have peace? That will ultimately determine what you allow to penetrate your spirit and how you move from this point forward. Here's the best part. If you make a mistake or a misstep, think of it more as a teachable moment. Get up and try again. The key is knowing that a lot of life may feel unfair, rough, discouraging, and extremely overwhelming. But even though it can be all of that in one day, and sometimes in one hour, everything is going to be ok. Selah.

You got this!

Christ gives me the strength to face anything.—Philippians 4:14 (CEV)

Mindfully Me

TODAY I WILL:

Epilogue

Every now and then a month has 31 days. So just in case you have an extra day this month and you're interested in another important lesson, here goes.

The earth can only harvest what you plant. The atmosphere will do the same thing. If you don't like what's going on in your world, then do something about it.

If you want to be loved, love. If you want to be celebrated, celebrate. If you want to be strengthened, strengthen. If you want to be appreciated, appreciate. If you want to be blessed, bless. If you want to be promoted, promote. What you release into the world will always find its way back to you. It's a principle. Just remember that you do not have control over when it comes back or from whom it will come. So stay open because just like you never know around which corner your fate lies, you never know who God is going to use to cause you to experience the return on your investment. Just a word of caution, it rarely comes back from the person or people to whom you've given it…and that's the best part. You begin to live your life in search of beautiful experiences from unexpected places.

Keep doing good because what you send out comes back. I promise.

> *A generous person will prosper; whoever refreshes others will be refreshed.—Proverbs 11:24 (NIV)*

I'M
PRAYING
FOR
YOU

ORDERED STEPS

MARICHAL MONTS

Just like my Father

MARICHAL B. MONTS

CPSIA information can be obtained
at www.ICGtesting.com
Printed in the USA
LVHW091922171220
674447LV00005B/62

9 781662 803475